PLEASE TAKE GOOD CARE OF YOUR BEST FRIEND!!

A Book on Pet Care

by Doris Day

TABLE OF CONTENTS

they leave it pure, they come so innocent and they go out innocent. You can't say that for people, but the animals maintain their innocence all the way through out their lives.

I mean inspired by their beauty, to take consideration, responsibility, and I do not many never go. And to that understand and happiness in the animals. To have a meal-time bond, a warm smile and a warm someone at home in the yard, or never return or a welcome in a cozy spot.

Through the years I've wondered why God put the animals here. When you think about life and lives

Preface

I guess you may be wondering when my devotion to my four-legged friends began. Actually, I can't remember a time when I didn't love critters! After being involved with Actors and Others for Animals for a number of years, I decided in 1977 to follow my heart and establish my own organization: the Doris Day Pet Foundation. Many of you may be members of the spin-off of this organization, the Doris Day Animal League.

Many times I am asked, "What inspires your love for animals?" The answer is really quite simple.

You can pick up a little mutt whom you've never seen before and be inspired by the love in his eyes, the depth of his soul, and the innocence and purity of his spirit. Animals come into this world pure and they leave it pure; they come in innocent and they go out innocent. You can't say that about people, but the animals maintain their spiritual beauty throughout their lives.

I'm also inspired by their joy. It seems to take considerable effort for people to find real joy and many never do. Animals, on the other hand, find happiness in the smallest pleasures—a pat on the head, a warm smile. They find pleasure in a ball game in the yard, a chewie by the fire, or a warm bed in a cozy spot.

Through the years, I've wondered why God put the animals here. When you think about the sad lives that many of them lead, you have to ask yourself that question. They have no rights. They are used for research. They are euthanized.

Why did God put the animals here? Well, I've come to this conclusion: I really believe that it was God's plan for us to learn from them and to emulate them. Maybe one day, people will wake up and realize what precious creatures animals are. Maybe one day, they will all be cherished and protected and valued for the perfect beings they are.

ACKNOWLEDGMENTS

My thanks and gratitude to Judy Ruby who has assisted me for many years in writing the advice columns from which this book was taken and Jamie Molitoris for her editorial skill in translating those columns into this book.

I also want to thank Dr. Steven Atwood of Animal Health Care Associates on Martha's Vineyard for his thoughtful review of the manuscript.

Illustrations by Kathy Raines

Author's Note

The recommendations and information provided in this book are intended to serve as a general guide regarding your pet's health and well-being, but they do not cover all information that may be available. After careful review, I have used my personal experience and knowledge to select the information that I feel is of the greatest use to you and your pet. While this book will enable you to deal with a wide range of situations, it is not a substitute for the medical advice and individualized diagnosis of particular symptoms that your veterinarian can provide. I recommend that you use this book to supplement regular visits with your veterinarian regarding your pet's health.

To make this project more consistent for my editor, I have decided that all references to our animal friends will be in the male gender—and that goes for references to veterinarians as well. It's easier and less confusing than seeing "he/she" in the text—but I want you to know that we are not ignoring the precious female of each species!

INTRODUCTION

As you read my book, please consider the following facts. I think you'll agree that we all need to take our responsibilities to our pets a bit more seriously.

- An estimated 52 million dogs and 57 million cats in this country are family pets.
- Millions of animals are euthanized in America's animal shelters each year.
- As many as 75% of all cats entering shelters are killed.
- As many as 61% of all dogs entering shelters are killed.
- As many as 25% of all dogs in shelters are purebreds.
- In just six years, one female dog and her offspring can produce 67,000 animals.
- In just seven years, one female cat and her offspring can produce 420,000 cats.
- For every human born, there are seven puppies and kittens born.

So, do your part, my friends. Spay or neuter your pets. Be certain they have proper ID. And be responsible pet caregivers. Pets are friends for life!!

Recommended Reading

I wouldn't be without my copies of the *Dog Owner's Home Veterinary Handbook* and the *Cat Owner's*

Home Veterinary Handbook by Delbert Carlson, M.D. and James Giffin, D.V.M., respectively. These books deal with day-to-day care as well as emergencies and they're extremely well-written.

The text is clear and simple and the photos and drawings show you exactly how to carry out instructions like giving a pill or applying ear medication. They're invaluable guides for every pet owner and I hope you'll look for them next time you're in a bookstore.

If you'd like to learn more about dog behavior, I recommend *When Good Dogs Do Bad Things*. Authors Mordecai Siegal and Matthew Margolis are true animal behavior experts and their book is chockfull of excellent information. Read this book as a preventative measure and to gain valuable insight into your dog's behavior.

There are also several good pet recipe books available, and two I suggest are *The New Natural Cat* by Anita Frazier, and *Natural Health for Dogs and Cats*, by Richard Pitcairn, D.V.M.

Finally, in the travel department, I recommend *Pets R Permitted*. This book not only lists hotels but also lists American Boarding Association kennels for day boarding along the way. It also has a national petsitter location service. And best of all, it's updated annually so you'll know the information is current. To make it even easier, you can order *Pets R Permitted* from the Doris Day Animal League.

Feeding Your Best Friend

THE IMPORTANCE OF DIET

1 Beauty—Not Just Skin Deep

Your pet's healthy skin and coat are a reflection of his overall well-being. Regular grooming—brushing, bathing and trimming—is essential, along with an excellent diet, regular exercise and routine health care.

Proteins, carbohydrates, fats, vitamins and minerals are specific nutrients that your pet needs to thrive, along with a constant supply of fresh, clean water. Commercially prepared diets have been formulated with your pet's nutritional requirements in mind. I wouldn't give my four-leggers anything but the highest quality foods and I stay away from generic brands. I always read the labels and look for a food that claims to be "nutritionally complete and balanced."

I feed a high-quality kibble and add a variety of pasta, vegetables, rice and grains that keep my Best Friends looking and feeling great.

I feel strongly that these home-cooked foods help keep my pets in excellent health, and a perfect example is my Honey Bun who, believe it or not, lived to be 22 years old! She resembled Benji, a blond beauty with lovely black markings. I rescued her when I lived in Los Angeles, and she wasn't even a year old.

2 Have You Hugged Your Dog Today?

Did you know that as many as 60 percent of all adult dogs are overweight or likely to get that way?

Every extra pound on a dog is proportionally greater than an extra pound on a human. For example, an extra five pounds on a dog that should ideally weigh 17 pounds is like adding 50 pounds to a person who should weigh 170. That's nearly 30 percent above their ideal weights!

Overweight dogs may be at higher risk for heart, respiratory and blood sugar level problems, skeletal stress and gastrointestinal disorders. Also, each pound of fat contains approximately 17 extra miles of blood vessels through which blood must flow, an unnecessary burden for the heart.

3 **Diet And Kidney Failure**

Kidney failure is the most common cause of death in older dogs. You can help to prevent this problem in your pet by becoming aware of your pet's changing dietary needs.

Diet is the single most important factor in slowing the aging process of the kidneys. To get your dog off to a good start, make sure your puppy receives a good diet early in life for normal kidney development. By mid-life, 7 to 8 years, a diet change should occur.

Your older dog will require less protein than a rapidly developing puppy. Only a certain amount of protein is required for normal tissue repair. Excess protein is broken down by the kidneys. It is this excess that works to shorten the normal life of the kidneys. To make sure that they aren't overworked, feed your older dog a high quality, low-protein diet. Ask your veterinarian to recommend a good one.

GETTING THEM TO EAT

4 **Don't Mix Foods**

Dog food is specially formulated for dogs, and cat food is made to fulfill a cat's nutritional requirements. Although an occasional nibble of your cat's food won't harm your dog and vice versa, cross-eating should be avoided if possible.

Feed your kitty on a counter or tabletop and keep his food away from your doggy. Cats require considerably more protein than dogs, and a long-term cat food diet would be bad for Fido. Also, cat food has much more fat than your dog requires. So—watch it!

5 Canine Feeding Tips

I feel it's just as important for our canine friends to have tasty, fresh, nutritious foods as it is for humans. Animals need and enjoy a varied and balanced diet, so don't think for a minute that your dog has to live on supermarket kibble and canned food. Supermarket brands may meet nutritional standards but we all know that fresh is best.

One of my dogs' favorite treats is stir-fried vegetables. I have a large wok in which I prepare these vegetables—and by the way, they're great-tasting so have a bowl yourself while you're preparing your pet's food. I use cold pressed sesame oil from the health food store. It's really delicious and great for your pet's skin. You may want to pre-cook the hard vegetables (like broccoli, turnips and carrots) in a steamer or microwave, or you can slice them paper-thin by hand or in a food processor. Then stir-fry, adding yellow crookneck and zucchini squash. Keep tasting until they're cooked just right. Brown rice or pasta makes a good starch to round out the meal.

The main reason I go into so much detail about how I feed my pets is because I want you to know that you don't have to spend a great deal of money to provide fresh, wholesome meals. Watch the sales, and when you're buying vegetables and pasta or rice for your family, just add a bit more for your four-legged kids.

6 Breakfast For Fido

Breakfast with your dog can be fun and easy. All you have to do is to feed Fido whatever you're having—as long as it's healthful food.

I give my older dogs a breakfast cereal like bite-size Shredded Wheat and they love it. This particular cereal has no salt, so it's good for my senior citizens. The younger dogs get Wheaties, Corn Flakes or any good granola cereal. Don't give them anything you wouldn't eat yourself—stay away from sweetened cereals with additives.

My dogs also love toast, and instead of butter, I use a low cholesterol spread. Peanut butter is another favorite with my gang. They like a little spread on their toast!

As you can see, when it comes to breakfast with

your Best Friend—if it's good enough for you, it's good enough for Fido.

7 Bedtime Snacks

Before your dog goes to sleep, it's a nice idea to give him a good quality doggy cookie from the pet store as a goodnight treat. These hard cookies are good for his teeth and gums, and your Best Friend will love having a nice bedtime snack.

Pet Fact

Unlike humans, your Best Friend doesn't need any vitamin C added to his diet. Dogs and cats are among the few animals whose bodies manufacture it!

---

8 Feline Feeding Tips

During the past few years, the nutrition of cats has received considerable attention. Certain large cat food manufacturers have conducted extensive research to establish complete, nutritious diets that require no supplementation.

Although federal law requires cat food manufacturers to provide a listing of ingredients in their products, the labels really don't contain enough information for you to comparison-shop. It's best to buy name brands from well-known manufacturers and stay away from generic or "plain wrap" varieties. When choosing a product, be sure to look for the words "complete, balanced, perfect or scientific" on the label. These words will tell you that the food meets all the daily protein, fat, vitamin, and mineral requirements for your cat.

A complete, high-quality kibble can be important to your cat's diet. It is abrasive and good for teeth and gums. The amount of ash (magnesium and phosphorus) your cat takes in each day is an important factor.

If you have a normal healthy cat, feed a *complete* kibble to be sure his nutritional needs are being met, then add some variety to his diet. (By the way, some cats will not eat kibble, and in that case, find a complete canned food.)

Cooked vegetables can be a special treat and can add some interest to your cat's diet.

If your cat suffers from FUS, watch the magnesium content or use a product recommended by your veterinarian. Most importantly, be moderate in feeding your cat. I feed mine twice a day and try to make their diet as interesting as possible without overfeeding. A "fat cat" runs the risks of many health problems, just like humans, so be kind to your kitty by

feeding the right amounts of wholesome, nutritious
foods.

Cats not only like to lie in the sun, they actually need sunshine to keep them healthy. It is
believed that the sun's rays produce vitamin D
on the cats' coats which they absorb when they
groom.

---

9 For The Birds

This winter, attract birds to your backyard with
taste-tempting treats made from a menu that will

satisfy a variety of feathered friends. Different species prefer to feed at different levels so secure food in trees, on stumps, in bird feeders, and in bushes. To get full enjoyment from bird watching, position the feeding stations near a window.

Listed below are a few edible suggestions for birds:

- String popcorn and cranberries on garlands and lace through shrubs or tree branches.
- Stuff large pinecones with peanut butter and roll them in cereal, cranberries or commercial bird seed.
- Mix bird seed, peanut butter and cornmeal with softened vegetable shortening. Spoon the mixture between the scales of pinecones, attach string and hang.
- Most birds enjoy bird cakes. To make this festive fare, blend 1 part peanut butter with 2 parts vegetable shortening. Harden in muffin tins, remove cakes and tie in mesh bags.
- Thread heavy cord through morsels of dates, orange sections and apple slices.
- Add enough cornmeal and birdseed to room temperature vegetable shortening to form a doughy mixture. Mold into a ball and place in the cavity of a tree or stump.
- You can also fill your bird feeder with finely cracked corn, peanut hearts or wheat.

• Hollow out one-half of a grapefruit or orange. Fill it with birdseed or unsalted peanuts. Hang on a tree limb.

10 More Food For Our Feathered Friends

Did you know that our feathered friends keep insect pests under control more than we realize? Although birds seldom eradicate a pest, they come close—and the effect is certainly friendlier to our environment than chemicals.

Robins, larks, quail, sparrows and blackbirds patrol the ground for insects, eggs and larvae. Even the often maligned crow eats bugs when he's not eating the farmer's corn. Blue jays eat more weed seeds and bugs than anything else.

There are many trees, shrubs and vines that provide shelter and food for the birds. Dogwood supplies food for as many as 86 species of birds (depending of course, on where you live). Cedar and pine trees offer dense protective cover and serve as winter windbreaks in colder climates. Holly berries are enjoyed by 45 species of birds. Seventeen species feed off the pyracantha's shiny orange-red berries.

Growing sunflowers is an easy and inexpensive way to feed the birds. They will attract as many as 40 species of seed-eating birds to your garden.

So, for your insect and weed control, and bird-watching pleasure, ask your nursery owner about vegetation you can plant to encourage our fine feathered friends.

NOT NECESSARILY FOOD

11 The Scent of Pleasure

Everyone knows that cats can go wild over catnip, but did you know they can be just as attracted to honeysuckle?

No one seems to know what it is about honeysuckle that makes cats react, but it affects the cat's sense of smell, giving them extreme pleasure through their olfactory nerves.

12 You Are What You Eat

"Pica" means the ingestion of non-food items. Our Best Friends have been known to swallow all sorts of strange objects, and many have the potential to cause serious problems.

The reason for your pet's interest in non-food items may be a medical problem, like a mineral deficiency in the diet. If your pet experiences indigestion or cramping, he might eat unusual things to try to "put out the fire." In that case, your veterinarian may sug-

gest a change in the pet's diet to ensure he eats a
high quality, nutritionally balanced food that's easily digested.

Behavioral problems can also be a cause. Pica may
be an offshoot of a chewing behavior. In that case,
training is essential so that your pet learns to respond
to your command to "drop" when he has something
undesirable in his mouth.

Pets are like children. Although accidents can happen, it's your responsibility to keep your Best Friend
safe—so keep those paper clips, rubber bands,
thumbtacks and other curiosities out of reach!

Enjoying Your Pets

PETS IN THE HOME

13 The Value Of Love—Don't Give Up Too Soon

Over the years I've received many letters from people who feel compelled to give up their beloved pets because of illness or a medical condition. Pregnant women have been told that cleaning a cat's litter box could endanger their babies; many senior citizens are fearful that a cat scratch could lead to serious health problems; people with fragile immune systems worry that pets could be a risk to their health.

Numerous studies confirm that pets are good for what ails us. We know that pet caregivers have stronger heartbeats than do non-pet caregivers, and the survival rate for patients with chronic diseases is higher for pet caregivers. Although some individuals may be more susceptible to some infections from some animals, giving up your Best Friend because you are worried about potential health risks isn't necessarily the right thing to do.

By taking some simple precautions, pet owners with serious medical conditions and compromised immune systems can keep their beloved pets. Here are some simple precautions to take:

- Avoid contact with a litter box, or wear rubber gloves, when changing the box.
- Wash your hands frequently, especially after changing a litter box or cleaning up after your pet.
- Maintain your pet's good health by providing preventative veterinary care.

Pets give us a reason for hope and they can mean the difference between hope and despair. Sometimes love is the best medicine of all.

14 Don't Get Your 'Dander' Up Over Cat Fur and Allergies

Contrary to popular opinion, cat fur does not cause allergies! However, cat saliva and dander can cause many problems.

When a cat grooms himself, he leaves behind a fine coat of saliva proteins on his fur. These proteins dry and fall on carpeting and furniture. Eventually they will cause a reaction in allergic people. Cat dander, extremely small scales in the cat's fur, acts the same way.

The best way to deal with these allergies is to rinse your cat once a month with distilled water to reduce the amount of dander. If you prefer not to thoroughly wet your cat, I've been told you can wipe your kitty each week with a towel soaked in distilled water, and that's just as effective. Groom your cat regularly and keep your house clean and well-vacuumed. Allergic family members should always wash their hands after touching or playing with cats.

15 Allergy Recipe

"Cat Fancy" magazine printed a wonderful recipe for readers who are allergic to their cats. It can be made by a veterinarian, as follows:

Mix 3 milliliters of 10 milligrams/milliliter of Acepromazine injectable in 27 milliliters of tap water. Give 12 drops to your cat once or twice daily in food. Acepromazine is a tranquilizer, but this dilution does not cause any drug effects. It does, however, change the character of the cat's saliva, making it less irritating to allergic humans.

Needless to say, you <u>must check with a veterinarian</u> before beginning any treatment. He will decide if your kitty-cat is a good candidate. Even homeopathic veterinarians have endorsed this treatment, because over a long period of time, there appear to be no side effects. They also realize that without some kind of relief for the caregiver, the kitty may become homeless.

16 Cleaner Air Can Help

Many people who have allergies find some relief by using ionizer/air cleaners. These efficient little machines help to remove dust, pollen and other particles from the air. And guess what—I understand they can be just as beneficial to an allergic cat or dog.

17 Cats And Cleaning

Here's a great tip for cleaning cat hair off carpeted cat toys like condos and scratching posts. Use a wire slicker brush! It works great and can also be used for quick clean-ups.

Many cat caregivers are allergic to their feline friends but that doesn't stop them from being cat caregivers. They must work extra hard to keep their surroundings as clean as possible, and that can mean eliminating carpet in favor of hardwood floors and tile, very limited use of fabrics, wearing dust masks while cleaning, using air purifiers to help eliminate allergens, and dusting, washing, sweeping, brushing (cats and furniture), mopping and vacuuming on a daily basis.

For general cleaning, I've heard very encouraging reports about water vacuums. Many people who have severe allergy problems, including allergy and asthma attacks, have noticed a real improvement in their condition when they use these gadgets.

18 Cat Scratch Disease

If you allow your kitty-cat to bite or scratch when you're spending time together, you may get more than you bargained for. Most cases of cat scratch disease (CSD) result from bites and scratches, and many victims are children.

Experts believe that CSD is caused by bacteria called rochalimaea.

It usually causes fever and swollen lymph nodes in the neck and armpits and a general feeling of malaise and fatigue. Although the symptoms are uncomfortable and tend to last for a while, the disease seems to be self-healing. Over time it runs its course, and most sufferers recover without needing medical intervention. Experts believe that once recovered, a person has a lifetime immunity to CSD.

Unfortunately, the symptoms can mimic those of more serious diseases like leukemia, tuberculosis and mononucleosis. The only way to make a conclusive diagnosis is through a lymph node biopsy.

CSD is seasonal. Most cases are reported between

July and January. Households with kittens are at greater risk, and the risk becomes higher if the kittens have fleas. Researchers don't yet understand what role fleas play in the transmission of CSD.

By using common sense and good hygiene you can minimize your chances of infection. So . . .

- Always wash your hands after handling your pet.
- If you are scratched or bitten, wash the area immediately with an antiseptic soap and see your doctor.
- Handle your kitty-cat gently and teach your children to do the same.
- Don't play rough.

19 Toddlers And Too Much Love

Indoor pets bring a new dimension to the lives of young children. Toddlers, however, can provide our four-leggers with "too much love." It's important for toddlers to be taught to respect animals from the very beginning.

Let your child know that there are appropriate ways to play—by throwing a ball or tugging a pull-toy, not by chasing or terrorizing kitty or doggie. If Fido is obedient on a leash, your child can take walks with you and learn to handle Fido. Be sure to use a harness, not a choke chain! The child can help you prepare kitty's meals and feed him and he can learn to watch kitty eat from a "safe" distance. Involve your child in your pet's daily care to teach him respect and kindness toward his Best Friend.

20 Shying Away From The Litter Box

There can be several reasons for a previously well-trained cat to suddenly choose not to use the litter box. He may have a health problem, so a medical check-up may be in order. It could be an emotional problem caused by spite, revenge, jealousy, or insecurity. The odor of urine or feces in the carpet may attract a previously trained cat and cause him to select this spot for future eliminations. Treatment depends on finding the cause and then taking steps to correct it.

A lapse in litter-box habits may be your cat's way of asking you to clean up your act. Many cats won't use a dirty litter box—and can you blame them?

Clean your cat's litter frequently. You should scoop out the solid waste a few times a day and completely replace the litter *at least* once a week—depending on how many cats you have.

Scrub litter pans with soap and water to keep them clean and fresh-smelling, and dry thoroughly before refilling. Again, this should be done once or twice a week, depending on how many cats live with you. *Never* sanitize litter boxes—or floors—using phenols or creosotes (such as PineSol), as these chemicals are life-threatening to cats. The cat's tender foot pads absorb the chemicals directly into the bloodstream at a higher level than the more callused foot pads of a dog.

Be sure to check the litter for indications of illness. Diarrhea and bloody stools, for example, could mean that your pet has parasites or other health problems.

Most veterinary behaviorists now recommend one litter box per cat in the household.

21 Why Does Your Cat Purr?

Why does your cat purr? Many say the answer is obvious: Cats purr because they are happy and contented. Surprisingly, that is not always true. Cats also purr when they are in pain, injured, in labor, and even dying. It seems that purring signifies a friendly social mood. In the case of a traumatized cat, it may indicate a need for friendship or, with a happy cat, it may be his way of saying thanks for kindness given.

22 The Nose Knows

The cat has his own social rituals. A case in point is the "nose knows" greeting. One cat approaches another with his tail standing straight in the air—a signal of friendly intent. If he isn't threatened, he will come closer and make nose-to-nose contact with the other cat. The ritual is executed very quickly, but it expresses deep trust as well as affection on the part of the initiating cat.

You can mimic this ritual by offering a finger or your own nose for your cat to touch. This seemingly small way of expressing affection for a feline friend is important and he may even respond in kind.

23 What To Do With An Untrained Puppy

Please don't send Fido to the garage at night just because he isn't housetrained yet. He is a member of your family and he should be warm, safe and cozy at night, just like your children.

I'm sure that your kitchen or utility room has a vinyl or tile floor, so what harm could possibly be done to that? If you can't confine him by closing the doors, get an expandable gate or make your own barrier. Put newspapers on the floor, provide some water and some puppy kibble (because puppies like to "nosh"), and make him a nice, warm bed with blankets. A ticking clock near his bed is comforting, too. He'll feel like part of the family, and you'll be training him at the same time. Take him out first thing in the morning and PRAISE him when he does his duty. After he's trained—I would hope that he'll be on your bed.

PETS OUTDOORS

24 Some Words Of Wisdom

Some weather can be hazardous to your pet's health—whether he's riding in the car, playing in the park or frolicking at the beach. Be especially aware of the effects of the hot summer sun, and avoid these common dangers:

- It's upsetting to see a dog forced to jog with his guardian. If the pet is leashed—as he should be— he must maintain his companion's pace. Your dog doesn't understand aerobics! He wants to stop and smell the flowers! Also, a mature dog ages at approximately seven times the human rate and could very well be too elderly to keep up with you. A good idea is to take him to the park or the beach, put him on a long expanded leash and let him fly around!

- Does your dog love to play in the surf? Then you should know that saltwater can make him seriously ill if he drinks too much. It's also bad for the skin, so watch it—take along fresh drinking water and rinse your pet's coat with clear water to avoid skin problems.

- Summer grasses can cause itchy rashes and make your pet miserable. Foxtails can burrow into ears, eyes, nose and even between his toes. Take a few minutes each day to thoroughly check for skin irritations. And don't forget those pesky fleas. Flea control is an absolute necessity during the summer months.

- Your pet may enjoy a dip in the pool, but don't allow it unless you're with him. In fact, it's imperative that you teach your dog to swim. Puppies should be kept away from the pool. They have no sense about water and they'll just fall in. You can teach your adult dog to swim by getting in the pool with him. Show him how to use the steps in the shallow end. Support his body, reassure him, steer him around, then take him back to the step and show him the way out. Repetition is the key, and if you are patient, he will learn quickly.

- Sunburn isn't just for humans. If your pet's nose has more pink areas than black, he's especially susceptible to burning and, just like humans, he can develop skin cancer. White cats and pets with fresh, short haircuts are also vulnerable. Apply a number 15 waterproof sunscreen often. Rub it in so that even if he licks it off, some already will have penetrated to protect his skin.

One more thing—and the most important to me— it's a scary thing to see someone throwing sticks or Frisbees far out into the water, then expecting the pet to retrieve them. If you don't know how treach-

erous surf can be, you do now! The waves are so
strong your pet could be carried out to sea. So heed
this advice and don't do it. Play on the sand, not in
the water.

25 On The Run

If you do decide to jog with your pooch, be certain
that your dog is physically capable of a work-out by
taking him to the veterinarian for a complete check-
up first. Remember that walking is just as beneficial
as running, and it doesn't put as much stress on the
system. If you're a jogger who cares for an older
pet, think about taking your exercise, then getting
out a leash and taking your dog for a nice, long walk.

If you share your home with a frisky, young pet
who *loves* to exercise, be sure to start your jogging
program at a modest pace and distance and build up
your pet's stamina as you would your own. As the
weather gets warmer, remember that taking your pet
for a run on a hot, humid day can be risky. Unlike
people, dogs can't sweat through their skin to control body temperature, so they may become over-
heated. Protect your pet by jogging during the cooler
morning or late afternoon hours.

Always exercise your dog on a leash and be careful to check his feet afterward for cuts, blisters, gravel
or thorns.

26 Warm Weather Warning:
No Dogs In The Car

Summertime's soaring temperatures call for you to make adjustments in your pet's routine. It's time to leave Fido at home when you go to the market, even though he enjoys shopping. The temperature inside a parked car can rise in minutes, causing your pet to suffer heatstroke, irreparable brain damage or death. Also, remember that even a shady spot can be unbearably hot.

It's far more comfortable for your doggy at home so please, think twice before taking him out in the hot summer months.

27 Beating The Heat

A children's plastic pre-formed wading pool can provide lots of fun for your Best Friend in the summer-time. With just an inch or two of water, it's safe and refreshing for your doggy to cool off on a warm day. Try it!

28 Cats Do Pant

We've all seen dogs panting to stay cool in the heat, but did you know that cats pant too? The only time I've seen my cats pant is when they're stressed—

either fearful or angry. However, according to my veterinarian, cats do indeed pant to cool off, but usually not until their environment is excessively hot—in the 100 degree or above range. Instead of panting, they attempt to lower their body temperature by licking their coats. As the saliva evaporates, they cool off.

29 Warm Weather Warning

In very warm weather, food spoils quickly, so get in the habit of leaving food out for a maximum of two hours. Toss what hasn't been eaten after that time.

Be sure to smell any canned food before you feed it to your Best Friend to be sure it's fresh. Even food kept in the fridge can be suspect in the summertime.

During times of hot weather it's also a good idea to give smaller amounts of food at more frequent intervals. It's a healthier way to eat, and you'll know your pet is always eating fresh food.

30 Baby, It's Cold Outside!

If your dog or cat could talk, he might be saying, "Please don't let me freeze!"

Your pets depend on you more than usual in the winter, so protect them from the cold and other wintertime dangers.

Here are a few tips:

- You need a coat in winter and so may your dog, especially if he's very young, very old or is not used to the cold. The coat or sweater should cover the dog's back as well as his chest. Measure from the neck to the base of the tail to determine the correct size.

- Keeping warm may mean eating more. Inside pets will generally get less exercise and gain weight, so feed them less—of course, all pets should be "inside pets" but if yours is outside he may need up to 25 percent more calories. A quality diet is needed to produce a good layer of fat.

- Wet fur is not warm fur! Towel dry your pet right away if he gets wet. Don't bathe pets in cold weather.

- Pet beds placed on floors are often chilly. Raise them off the floor a few inches and keep them away from doors and windows.

- Winter shelters should be dry, warm and draft-free. It's also important to elevate them a few inches so they stay dry in wet weather.

- Pets need fresh water twice a day. An inside pet may need more because of dry, heated air.

- An active animal is healthier and happier. Exercise and play with your Best Friend a lot!

31 Don't Start Your Engines

Too often we read of injuries to kitty-cats who were sleeping on a car engine when it was started by an unsuspecting motorist. Please keep your kitty-cat inside and keep your car in the garage. If you have to park outdoors, thump the hood or beep the horn to warn sleeping cats before starting the engine.

32 Antifreeze/Coolant Additive

Ethylene glycol is the active ingredient—and deadly poison—in most antifreezes/coolants. A safer alternative is propelyne glycol, which is significantly less toxic and can be found in several antifreeze products including Sierra antifreeze/coolant.

Additionally, there exists a chemical called Bitrex that, when added to antifreeze, makes it unappealing to both children and animals. This product is widely used in Europe and is well-tested. It doesn't interfere with the effectiveness of antifreeze and it won't harm your vehicle.

To help insure the safety of both pets and children, store sealed antifreeze containers away and promptly clean up any spills.

ACCIDENTS <u>DO</u> HAPPEN!

33 Little Messes

Everyone has an accident now and then! If your four-legger makes a puddle on the carpet, here are some tips for stain removal:

- Using a paper towel, quickly blot up as much of the liquid as you can.
- Pour a little white vinegar on the stain, either straight or mixed 50-50 with water. Then blot it up, always working inward so you don't make the stain larger. You may have to moisten the stain three or four times until you remove it completely.
- Sprinkle cornstarch or baking soda onto the area and work it in. It will help absorb the moisture and odor. Wait four to six hours, then vacuum.
- For a really difficult stain, mix one tablespoon of ammonia with one teaspoon of liquid dishwashing detergent in a quart of cold water. Pre-test on a corner of the carpet, then work it into the stain, blotting to lift the moisture and odor.

34 Slippery Floors

Hardwood and tile floors are wonderful when you have pets. Clean-up is a breeze compared to carpeting and you know when they look clean, they are clean!

However, older dogs, in particular, have a hard time getting around on those slick surfaces. They no longer have the strength and agility to navigate, and a fall on a hard floor can cause real damage—and fear. Pressure sores and calluses can also be a problem.

I've used runners made from lengths of carpet to help my senior citizens get around, and they know exactly what the carpet is for! Also, if you keep their toenails clipped close it helps them grasp the floor more easily.

KEEPING A CHECK ON YOUR PETS

35 Training Collars

If you are struggling to train your puppy or young dog to walk on a lead, a choke chain may be the logical choice, right? Wrong!

Many knowledgeable trainers and veterinarians realize that the choke chain is a dangerous relic of the dark ages of dog training that is potentially dangerous in both expert and inexpert hands. A strong jerk has been known to cause an eye hemorrhage to a Doberman, supposedly a very "strong-neck" breed. Furthermore, the jerking motion can cause permanent damage to your pet's neck. If your dog becomes frightened and tries to bolt over a fence, the choke chain can get caught, and your dog will hang himself.

Response to many complaints about the choke collar has resulted in a number of versions of canine head collars. One version is based on a dog's natural instinct to pull against pressure, but it puts the pressure on the back of the neck and away from the front of the throat. The designers took a tip from canine mother nature; a puppy responds to control from its mother when she puts pressure on the scruff of its neck.

36 Pet Collars: The Good And The Bad

You can walk into any pet shop and see collars in every style, size, and color imaginable. But don't be an impulse buyer when it comes to this very important item for your pet. Just because your neighbor's Rottweiler sports a studded leather collar, doesn't mean it is the proper thing to wear. Leather collars can bind and be uncomfortable and even more importantly, they're an animal by-product, and why should we support that?

Your pet should *always* wear a collar with an ID tag. I recommend adjustable, nylon collars. They're about 1/2 to 3/4-inch wide. You can poke your own holes in the smaller sizes for a perfect fit, and they come in every color under the sun. They'll fit neck sizes from the tiniest to the largest dog, and they're just perfect for everyday wear. For your kitty-cat, you should purchase a nylon collar with an elastic insert to allow him to escape if the collar is caught.

When you go for a walk, you'll need more control over your pet and I heartily recommend a harness. Every collar made will put stress on your pet's neck when he needs to be restrained. A harness fits over your pet's body and there's no stress anywhere. They come in all sizes and in fashionable colors, too. So do your pet a favor—pick up a nylon collar and harness ASAP and remember to use that ID tag.

37 Reminder: Collar Check

Always remember that as your puppy or kitten grows, you must check his collar weekly to make sure it hasn't become too snug. A pet usually outgrows his first collar, and a collar that's too tight will irritate his skin and be very uncomfortable.

ALWAYS ADJUST YOUR PET'S COLLAR SO THAT YOU CAN EASILY SLIP TWO FINGERS UNDER IT.

38 **It's Never Too Early To Train Your Puppy**

Years ago, when dog training methods were fairly negative and sometimes harsh, it was commonly believed that a young puppy was too fragile and insecure to be "taught." By the time he was six months of age, when training usually began, the average dog had experienced plenty of negative learning. That meant he ignored his trainer, was totally confused and had many bad habits.

We now know that puppies are like little sponges, ready and willing to learn. The ideal time to bring a puppy into your home is at eight weeks of age. This is the time when he begins to bond, and you can immediately begin teaching him desired behaviors.

Between the ages of eight and 10 weeks, the puppy goes through a stage called the *fear imprintment* period. He is just learning to trust, and his fragile little ego can be damaged easily. Since this is about the time you'll be trying to housetrain, the correct approach is vitally important.

The third and fourth months of a puppy's life are called the *socialization* period, and during this time it is crucial for puppies to receive proper socialization and training if they are to mature into calm, confident, well-rounded adults. They should have lots of positive exposure to a variety of strangers, other dogs and different environments.

Today the concept of puppy kindergarten is sweeping the country. It should be a gentle, positive approach in learning and problem prevention.

I know I've talked about training a lot. The reason for this focus is all those sad little faces, waiting in cages in animal shelters. Thousands and thousands are euthanized because they have become uncontrollable, temperamental, aggressive, anti-social, fearful, nervous or "untrainable" adults.

If your family includes a puppy—or if you plan to adopt one in the future—please take the time to attend a reputable training class. The National Association of Dog Obedience instructors is interested in improving dog obedience training and instruction. For information about this organization or the name of the NADOI instructor nearest you, contact NADOI, 2286 E. Steel Road, St. John, MI 48879. Give your puppy a chance to be the best he can be!

39 Socializing The Shy Dog

Is your dog a shrinking violet? Does he cower when called and find it difficult to interact with people and fellow pets? Does he overreact to noise or seem fearful? Try to coax him out of the closet with these tactics:

- *Fun runs.* Take your leashed dog with you on walks or short visits to friends. Limit the outings to 10 or 15 minutes initially, gradually increasing his time outside.

• *Social training*. Group obedience classes expose bashful pups to people and other pets, while teaching them that their caregivers' actions are predictable.

• *Words of approval*. Reward your dog's positive behavior with petting and lavish praise.

THE NOT-SO-GREAT OUTDOORS

40 Outdoor Dogs

Once while visiting a friend, I heard a dog barking. It wasn't the bark of a dog protecting his home; it was a pitiful, mournful sound that I'd heard many times before.

When the barking didn't stop after a few minutes, I went to the deck and looked out—and the sight was a familiar one to me. A beautiful medium-sized shepherd-mix was chained to a tree, his water bowl knocked over, weeds and dirt all around, children's toys strewn about the yard. His chain was not long enough to allow access to the patio where a doghouse and dirty rug were probably his nighttime sleeping quarters.

Why do people have "outdoor" dogs? I guess it's for convenience and because they desire a certain amount of separation from their pets. After all, it's just easier to leave them outside rather than have them indoors where they are underfoot and cause a multitude of problems with fleas and allergies, dirt and odors. Dogs are animals and animals belong outside, right?

Wrong, wrong, wrong! Dogs are domesticated animals. They live and breathe for their human friends, and they will gladly risk their lives to protect that bond.

My four-leggers are the best part of my life. They bring laughter and joy, peace and serenity, and a great sense of purpose and responsibility to my life. I learn incredible lessons from them every single day—lessons in loyalty, unconditional love, gratitude, and forgiveness. There is so much to learn from our non-human friends and when I see those who aren't given the opportunity to share, I know why they cry.

41 **Indoor vs. Outdoor Cats**

Cats who are allowed to roam loose outdoors generally die young. When I've tried to explain this sad fact, people always tell me they *can't* keep their kitty-cat indoors. He meows, he cries, he looks longingly out the window with big, sad eyes.

Believe me, I know how much cats love being outdoors, but if they could comprehend the dangers out there, I'm sure they would choose to stay inside.

Almost all of the injuries and illnesses that occur in cats are the *direct result* of being allowed to roam outdoors. Everyday, veterinarians see broken legs, fractured pelvises and internal organ traumas in cats who were struck by vehicles. Is it worth it?

Abscesses and fight wounds are the result of battles for territory. Cats are rather solitary creatures who may stake out an area several hundred yards around their living quarters. They will attempt to keep this area clear of any invading felines and vicious battles, sometimes to the death, are not uncommon. Is it worth it?

These aggressive interactions among cats also promote the spread of contagious diseases. Feline Leukemia Virus Infection (FELV), Feline Immunodeficiency Virus (FIV or cat AIDS) and other severe upper respiratory infections are easily spread through bite wounds and, although your cat can be vaccinated against some of these diseases, he is still vulnerable to many others. There is no vaccine for FIV, and many veterinarians question the reliability of FELV vaccine.

Aside from these natural dangers, cats suffer even more from the greatest danger of all—humans. A wandering, curious feline who may dig or soil in someone's garden, or snoop in their trash cans, or spray on their shiny chrome hubcaps may suffer frightening consequences. Is it worth it?

The principle of preventative medicine certainly applies here. All of the problems I've mentioned are virtually 100 percent avoidable if we keep our little furry Best Friends safe and content indoors. Your veterinary bills will be considerably less and you can look forward to many happy days with your feline friend. Please, think about it.

42 Bringing Outdoor Cats In

Making an outdoor cat an indoor cat can become a battle of wills in the early stages. Once you make the decision to bring your kitty inside, you must keep him inside permanently. By allowing him outside, even for short periods, you are rewarding him for showing his desire to go out. Do not allow him out at all! Ignore him completely when he asks to go out. If you can be strong for a couple of days, he will probably stop the asking-to-go-out behavior. All of mine live in and they all came to me as outdoor cats. They never show a sign that they would rather be outdoors, so hang in there!

43 Runaway Dogs

Many times, dogs who haven't been neutered are very anxious to leave the confines of their own domain to go explore the world beyond. It is very important for health *and* safety reasons that you have your dog neutered.

If your dog has been neutered and still tends to run away from your yard, you may need to check your fencing. Six-foot fences keep most dogs in and you can usually add some sort of "temporary" material (like lattice) on top of that without violating building codes.

If that doesn't work, you should consider building a chain link dog run. If you have to leave your house for an extended period of time and can't confine Fido indoors, the run will give shelter (of course it must be roofed) and keep him safe. Unfortunately, dog runs are often misused, and many pets end up spending their lives in a cage. Dog runs should be used only to keep your dog safe when he can't be with you.

44 Keeping Unwanted Friends Out

Pet doors are a real necessity to help our Best Friends go into and out of our homes freely. Many people have experienced the downside of pet doors which is the easy entrance of our wild four-legged friends into our homes. I have learned a tried-and-true method for preventing raccoons from using my pet door.

Cut a piece of chicken wire to place on the ground

directly in front of the pet door. Staple it on opposite ends to pieces of 2x4 to keep the chicken wire in place. At night, position the chicken wire mat in front of the pet door. It won't harm the raccoons or your pets, but raccoons won't walk on the wire because of their long claws. Your cat or dog will quickly become accustomed to the wire.

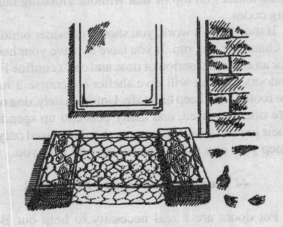

45 Taming The Wild Beast

Our Best Friends can become quite destructive when they're bored. I've heard from many cat caregivers whose indoor pets have really "raised the roof" because they were looking for fun and excitement. Many owners complain that they spent a fortune on cat toys, and their cats still tore up furniture and draperies. The secret is finding something that will interest your cat, and what works today may not be so exciting next week.

Well, I have some suggestions that should stimulate and entertain your feline friends. Have you seen "cat dancers?" They look like fishing poles with feathers or colorful objects dangling from the end. These are really terrific exercisers, mentally and physically challenging, and lots of fun for you and your cat. Don't let small children play with these, and be sure to put them out of sight when the game is over.

Cardboard boxes with holes cut in the sides make great hiding places, as do brown paper grocery bags.

We all know that bird-watching ranks as one of a cat's favorite activities. Now you can buy perches that mount under windows so your kitty-cat can spend endless hours snoozing in the sun or enjoying the view.

With a little time and ingenuity you really can keep your kitty-cat on the right track. If you're a handy person, try building a cat tree. A post covered with burlap or another heavy fabric or made of soft pine offers a good alternative to your furniture. The post should be sturdy and tall enough so that your cat can stretch to his full length while using it.

Introduce your pet to the post by stroking his paws

against it. To be sure he'll use it, scent the post with catnip and position it near a place where he likes to scratch. If you catch him clawing something that is off-limits, stop him with a firm verbal command accompanied by a loud clap. Then take him immediately to his scratching post and praise him while he uses it. Be patient and kind and your kitty should get the idea.

You may also want to recycle your aluminum foil by making it into a toy your kitty will love. Take a sheet of aluminum foil and shape it into a tight ball about the size of a ping-pong ball. I've found that kittens absolutely love to play with this "toy." They jump on it, grab it and roll around, bite it, bat it and just have a grand time. It's fun to watch them too, so be sure to try this one—but only with your supervision. Extended play could cause the foil ball to tear or come apart and ingestion of the foil could cause health problems.

Many cats enjoy a walk outdoors. It will take a little time and patience to accustom your cat to a chest harness and leash but it can be done!

Of course, I always say that having two cats is better than having just one. My cats love to play together. They frolic all day and cuddle at night so my best advice is always—take two!

46 Natural Cat Repellent

If your kitty-cats have a habit of napping on the kitchen table, or if they take a particular delight in shredding your wicker trunk, I have an idea that might work for you—try using eucalyptus oil; a natural repellent to cats.

Place a few drops of oil, where it won't leave a stain, on furniture or fabrics. A bowl of potpourri saturated with oil can be placed on counters, table-tops, or any place you would like to discourage your cats from using as a rest stop. A cotton ball soaked in eucalyptus oil works well inside a place like the aforementioned trunk. This simple trick can be a pleasant, non-toxic solution for undesirable behaviors.

47 Beds For Pets

If your pet usually sleeps with you and you're worried about his falling off the bed, you may want to invest in a child's playpen. Second-hand shops are great places to begin your search for a reasonably priced one. You can make your own bumper from soft blankets to create a perfect place for your older doggies to rest.

This is also a great idea if your pet has stitches from a surgery, or if he isn't feeling well and needs to be kept quiet and apart from the rest of the family. It gives you peace of mind to have a nice safe place for your doggie and gives him a great sense of security and safety.

DISASTER READY

48 Fire Rescue

When a blaze burns quickly and ferociously, there is little time to ensure the safety of family pets.

Before it's too late to protect your pet in the event of a fire, you should purchase and display Pet Alert stickers. These stickers are displayed by your front and back doors, and tell firefighters how many and what kinds of pets may be inside. These stickers are available through the Doris Day Animal League, in pet stores and through pet supply catalogues. I strongly urge you to shop for some, and choose a style that's brightly colored with enough space for each pet's name and description.

49 Prepare For Disaster

You never know when disaster will strike, so the best thing to do is to be prepared for anything. To help your pet find his way home in a disaster, please make sure he always wears his collar and ID tags.

This may be the only way your precious friend will find his way home again. Also, keep handy a current photo of your pet. If he should become lost, you can use the picture to make flyers.

Keep an animal first aid book and emergency kit handy. These are available in many pet supply stores. Be certain vaccination records are current in case you need to find a boarding facility on short notice. Many kennels will not accept pets without proof of vaccinations. Also, be sure you know how to administer pet CPR and the Heimlich Maneuver.

The best advice I can give is to be prepared. Always keep a two-week food and bottled water supply—for yourself and for your pets. If your pet takes medication regularly, have at least one week's supply on hand. Keep your pet indoors at night.

A few simple precautions can prevent a tragedy.

BIRDWATCHING

50 Backyard Birds

Bird-watching from your own window or backyard can bring endless hours of pleasure. Here are some tips for attracting our feathered friends:

• Place feeders off the ground so birds will be safe from dogs and cats.

- To attract a wide variety of birds, mix birdseed with other treats like bread, granola, chopped fruit, raisins and shelled peanuts.
- Once you start feeding, don't stop! The birds will depend on you, especially in the winter when food is scarce.
- Don't put out more than two cups of food per day.
- Make your own birdbath by turning a trash can lid upside-down on a stand. Keep the water fresh and wash the birdbath weekly.
- Help birds clean their plumage by providing a shallow box filled with fine, washed sand. They will use this sand to dust their plumage.

51 Wild Bird Feeders

Millions of birds die each year from window strikes. Most of the birds are killed while approaching bird feeders located near windows.

Deterrents like decals placed on the glass and moving objects hung from the window don't prevent collisions because the windows reflect vegetation and camouflage these objects. Many times the birds avoid the objects but still hit the window. Bird feeders should be placed far enough away from your home so they won't attract birds to the hazard of closed windows.

Beware—Hazards In And Around The Home

> **In emergencies, help is available for your pet through the National Animal Poison Control Center: 1-800-548-2423.**

52 Heimlich Maneuver

Did you know that the Heimlich Maneuver can be used to dislodge an object stuck in the throat of your dog or cat? Here are the basic instructions:

The animal must be upright, facing in the same direction you are. Place your arms around him with your hands overlapping at the animal's underchest. Apply quick, sharp pressure where the breastbone meets the abdomen.

This motion causes sudden compression of the chest cavity, forcing air out of the lungs against the object in the windpipe; hopefully dislodging it.

Please ask your veterinarian to demonstrate this life-saving technique the next time you and your Best Friend pay a visit.

HOLIDAY HAZARDS

53 A Safe Halloween

Witches, ghosts and goblins will haunt our neighborhoods during Halloween, but this festive time is anything but fun for our four-legged friends.

They can find the presence of so many strangers threatening and confusing. The noise and costumes create even more of a problem. Your dog may be friendly and his behavior predictable, but on Halloween, feeling protective of his home, your Best Friend may become aggressive or frightened. Cats are highly sensitive animals and any change in routine can cause them to become very agitated. Your kitty could easily dart out the door—and you may not even be aware he's missing until hours later.

For a truly happy Halloween, try these hints:

• Confine your pet to a quiet room and look in on him from time to time to reassure that all is well. An outdoor pet should certainly be kept indoors for the night.

• Be sure your pet is wearing a collar and ID tag just in case he gets out.

- Keep all Halloween candies away from your pet, and remember to carefully dispose of any wrappers or sticks after you eat a treat.
- Don't dress your pet in a costume. It's confusing and upsetting to most animals. If you go out trick-or-treating or if you accompany your children around the neighborhood, leave your pet at home.
- Black cats may be in danger because of their association with this holiday. Take extra precautions to protect your kitty-cat from pranks or mistreatment by keeping him inside.

54 No Bones Please

If turkey will be a part of your Thanksgiving meal, remember that excessive amounts of turkey meat—or fat—can be difficult for your pet to digest and can cause intestinal upset. Also, some animals may develop allergic reactions to foods they aren't accustomed to eating.

If turkey is a regular part of the diet of your pets, they can certainly share in your meal. Otherwise, be very careful.

Turkey bones are hollow so they are very brittle and splinter easily. If swallowed, a sharp piece can puncture the intestines or cause a blockage. Symptoms may not appear for a day or two. So, NO BONES PLEASE.

Salmonella poisoning is another danger to pets and to people. Salmonella bacteria live in the intestinal tract of turkeys and other animals. Cooking usually destroys the bacteria but if the turkey meat is undercooked, (and that can happen at the center of the turkey if it's full of stuffing), you can have problems.

Salmonella bacteria can multiply and cause contamination if the meat sits at room temperature for too long. Any person, or pet, eating the contaminated meat is at risk of poisoning, so beware.

Symptoms of salmonella poisoning include stomach upset, diarrhea, vomiting, fever, loss of appetite and listlessness. If your pet shows any of these signs and has eaten from the table, contact your veterinarian immediately.

55 Dangerous Leftovers

One last reminder about Thanksgiving hazards. Many pets are attracted to the twine used to truss turkeys and to the small pop-up thermometers often found in turkeys bought at the supermarket.

They smell and taste like turkey meat, so your Best Friend may raid the garbage to get into these "leftovers." That twine can be absolutely deadly to your pet! It can wrap around the intestines and cause a serious intestinal blockage that could result in death.

The plastic thermometer can cause similar damage, so after you've cleared the holiday table, put all of the garbage into a secure container and lock it away from your precious pet.

56 Holiday Safety Tips (Sights and Smells)

The beautiful plants and flowers that make the December holiday season so special can also injure your pet. The red or white leaves of a poinsettia produce a sap that can irritate an animal's skin and upset his tummy if eaten. Holly berries, or castor beans, can be extremely poisonous and symptoms may not appear for 18-24 hours. Mistletoe is very dangerous to pets; all parts of the plant are toxic, but the berries are especially poisonous. Christmas rose and Star-of-Bethlehem should be kept well out of reach.

Prevent your pet from drinking harmful Christmas tree water by covering the stand and never adding chemical preservatives to the water. Keep the tree fresh by watering as needed. When your tree does begin to dry out, don't leave fallen pine needles on the floor. They're not only sharp but also toxic and have been known to cause internal damage.

Be sure to secure the tree properly so it can't be knocked over. Tie fishing line at the top and fasten it to a hook in the ceiling, tie it to a railing or secure it to a banister. Screw the tree base to plywood for more support.

Sweets, cakes and cookies are human snacks and can upset an animal's metabolic balance, leading to serious illness. The same is true for spilled alcoholic beverages your pet may lap up. Splintery bones and fat from holiday meals are no-nos, too.

Chocolate is a particularly dangerous pet poison because it contains theobromine, a powerful stimulant that is toxic to pets. All types of chocolate contain theobromine, but dark chocolate has the highest concentration. *Believe it or not, as little as 2 ounces of dark chocolate can kill a 10 pound dog!* Chocolate can poison cats too, although cats rarely eat chocolate.

If you think your pet has eaten a poisonous substance, call your veterinarian or poison control center immediately, even if you see nothing alarming right away. Symptoms may not appear until the next day and by then, it may be too late to save your pet's life.

57 More Holiday Safety Tips
(Baubles and Beads)

When you're wrapping gifts, be sure your pets don't run off with the yarn or ribbon. They can cause *serious* intestinal damage. Shiny tinsel, so attractive to kitty-cats, poses a similar threat so keep the tinsel high on the tree where it's harder to reach.

All breakable ornaments should hang near the top of the tree. Ceramic ornaments with lead glaze or sprayed-on "snow" can be toxic. Try using loops of ribbon to hang your ornaments; wire ornament hooks can be deadly.

Turn the Christmas tree lights off when the room is unattended. Curious puppies and kittens will be attracted to all the strings and wires lying around, and those can be fatal chew toys. Keep them out of your pet's reach. Better yet, cover them, tack them down, or spray them with a deterrent like Bitter Apple (available at pet supply shops). A tabletop tree would be better than one on the floor; however, many folks like tall trees, so please watch your pets carefully.

58 Holiday Heat Hazards

During the holidays, many people like to use their fireplaces and may be using their kitchen appliances more often than normal. In the hustle and bustle of the holidays, we may forget to take a few extra precautions to keep our Best Friends safe from these hot hazards.

Your Best Friend will probably enjoy the warmth and light provided by a nice fire in the fireplace. Keep him from being singed by using a sturdy, protective screen in front of the opening.

If your curious kitty-cat likes to check out the kitchen counters, remember that hot baking pans and other hot dishes can burn feet and noses. Place these hot items well out of kitty's reach.

If you're planning a holiday party, the best way to protect your pet from all of these hazards is to confine him to a quiet, safe room away from the hustle and bustle. Look in on him frequently and reassure him that all is well.

INDOOR HAZARDS FOR YOUR PETS

59 Watch Those Windows

Upper-story window ledges and balconies can be dangerous lounging spots for dogs and cats. Ruptured lungs, broken bones or teeth, and torn spleens or bladders are some of the injuries animals have sustained in accidents such as falls from high places.

Please don't put your pets in danger! Keep windows screened or closed, and supervise your pet when he's taking a siesta on the terrace.

60 Chewing Houseplants Is In Bad Taste

Curiosity killed the cat, or so they say, and that's especially true when it comes to our pets nibbling poisonous houseplants. Your pet may swallow part of a toxic plant and survive with no significant problem, but that's just luck. Your pet's tolerance depends on the type of toxin in the plant and the amount ingested, as well as the size and weight of your pet.

Protect your pet from a plant poisoning tragedy by making your home as safe as you would for your child. It's easy enough to keep plants out of Fido's reach, but a mischievous feline friend will find a way to reach them. Try treating the tips of the leaves with powdered ginger. This method is safe for both pets and plants and the unpleasant taste provides a good deterrent. Mist the plant first, then apply the powder to the leaf tips with your fingers. Reapply as necessary.

Instead of using a saucer, water your plants at the sink and let them drain. Otherwise, your pet may drink water that is standing in a saucer and become ill from the fertilizer.

Teach your pet that dirt isn't for digging and pots aren't for tipping. Make sure your plants are firmly rooted in heavy wide-bottomed containers. Cover the soil of any problem plants with rough decorative rock.

Safe houseplants for your animals include: Chinese Jade, Hawaiian Ti, African Violet, Creeping Charlie, Swedish Ivy, Baby Rubber Plant, Fishtail Fern, Ladder Fern and Boston Fern. Among the toxic plants are: Oleander, Hydrangea, English Ivy and Caladium. If any of the plants in your home or yard present a threat, replace them with something safer.

In emergencies, help for your pets is available through the National Animal Poison Control Center: 1-800-548-2423.

A veterinary toxicologist staffs the phone and the center is open 24 hours a day, 365 days a year. If it is determined that veterinary help is necessary, calls are subject to a charge, payable by VISA or Mastercard. Based on the information you give over the phone, you can receive immediate first-aid instructions and recommendations for short-term treatment. You can also call your veterinarian. The center offers veterinarian-to-veterinarian medical advice for those pets taken directly to clinics.

61 Twist Tie Warning

A cat was taken on an emergency trip to his veterinarian because he was in obvious distress. He wouldn't eat or drink and he was inactive and listless. His white blood count was elevated, indicating a severe infection. A full body X-ray revealed two wires twisted together in his small bowel.

Emergency surgery was performed and the culprits turned out to be two twist ties from bread bags!

To prevent a twist-tie tragedy, replace all wire closures with plastic tab closures or, better yet, use plastic bread-saver containers—and self-closing garbage bags.

62 No Aluminum Please

In a pinch, do you ever feed your pet from an aluminum pan? Be aware that he can be severely cut if he chews on the pan. It's best to feed your Best Friend in a nice crockery-type bowl. They're heavy enough to stay put, they won't slide, and they can't be chewed.

63 Plastic Warning

Our animal friends don't have hands, so it's often impossible for them to free themselves when they get stuck. Plastic is a real danger whether it's in the form of fishing line, plastic rings that hold soda and beer cans together, fishing nets, plastic sacks or net bags. So be a lifesaver—recycle plastic when you can; otherwise, put it in a trash can and do your part by picking up plastic when you see it on the beach or at the park.

64 Dental Floss Dangers

Kitty-cats are mischievous little critters and sometimes their curiosity can get them into big trouble. Wastebaskets seem to be particularly interesting, and those in the bathroom can hold some fairly dangerous items.

Dental floss is usually tossed into the wastebasket without a thought. But did you know that it can wrap around internal organs and cause serious—sometimes fatal—damage?

The same thing can be said about sewing thread, so please make sure these items are far out of your Best Friend's reach.

By the way, Q-tips are another "delicacy" and, as you can imagine, they aren't easily passed. Beware of what you toss!

65 Box Springs Can Be Bad News

Have you checked the underside of your box spring lately? Many kitty-cats like to shred and play with the cotton batting that covers the underside of box springs, and ingestion of this material is often the cause of chronic vomiting problems. How's this for a simple solution—put a fitted sheet on the under-side of your box spring!

66 Safety First

Kitty cats definitely like to keep us on our toes, so we have to do our best to stay one step ahead of them.

Please, always remember to check your washer and dryer for a napping feline, and the same goes for open dresser drawers. Here are some more tips to ensure your cat's safety.

- Recliners, sofa beds and fold-away beds provide a dark, cozy place for a siesta. Check the open space under these kinds of furniture before folding them up.
- Venetian blind cords can strangle a cat. You can avoid this tragedy by installing a hook on the wall and wrapping the cord around it.
- An ironing board can easily fall over if your cat jumps on it. A hot iron can cause serious injury. If you're interrupted while ironing, be sure your kitty is elsewhere and close the door to that room.
- Cats lick their paws. When you use a chemical product in your home, keep your cat out of the room you are cleaning until you are certain all surfaces are dry and no residue remains. Baking soda is a nontoxic substance you can use as a scouring agent. Rinse with vinegar and water for a clean, fresh scent that won't harm your pets or the environment.
- Insecticides and gardening chemicals can be deadly if your cat walks through them and then licks his paws. There are lots of environmentally safe products on the market, but I still feel uneasy about my animals being around them when they're freshly applied. Another good reason to keep your cat *indoors!*

• Sewing needles, pins, nails and other small, sharp objects can seriously harm your cat if swallowed.

When he was just a kitten, Smudge, one of my collaborator's cats, jumped onto Judy's desk, stood up on her typewriter on his hind legs, and pulled the pushpins out of the bulletin board on the wall. Judy couldn't figure out how those pushpins got on the floor that day, but she quickly removed all of them. That evening she went into her office to find Smudge up on the typewriter, looking for more pushpins. She tried using tape but soon learned that Smudge's mission was to *clean* the bulletin board. Now things are as they should be—according to Smudge. The bulletin board is empty and he still stands on the typewriter, using the bulletin board as a scratching post!

I have one last thought that I've expressed before and it's about keeping your cat indoors. If you have an outdoor cat, you probably don't have a litter box inside. That means you can't be aware of a very serious problem your cat may be experiencing—blood in the urine or stool. This can be a sign of a number of very serious conditions that should be treated immediately. There are so many reasons to keep your cat indoors: traffic, other animals, people, disease. Think about it and do what's right for your Best Friend.

67 Birdcage Warning

Antique birdcages may be pretty to look at, but they can be poisonous to birds. Such cages were often painted with lead-based paint, and the rusting wires may contain zinc. Both metals are toxic to our feathered friends.

Play it safe—use the antique cage for show, and buy Tweety the new galvanized metal home he deserves. And don't forget to wash the cage before you use it.

OUTDOOR HAZARDS FOR YOUR PETS

68 Grazin' In The Grass

Does your dog like to munch on grass? No one seems to know exactly why some canines occasionally snack on grass, but there are lots of theories.

Some experts say they simply enjoy the taste and texture. Others suspect it may be a substitute for the semi-digested plants that the dog's wolf cousins obtain from eating their prey's digestive organs. Still others think that dogs eat grass to induce vomiting to relieve an upset stomach. Whatever their reason for eating grass, dogs cannot digest it because it contains mostly cellulose fiber. That's why grass usually exits the dog in the same form it entered!

Though grass-eating is usually harmless, you should be aware that there are potential problems. Many lawns are treated with pesticides or fertilizers that could be dangerous to your dog. The eggs of intestinal parasites—like hookworms, whipworms and roundworms—can be found in grass and your pet could become infected.

To wean your dog off grass, some veterinarians suggest adding steamed vegetables to your dog's regular diet (avoid onions, which in large quantities can be toxic to dogs). Steaming vegetables breaks down some of the fiber, so they're easier to digest but still flavorful and crunchy.

My four-leggers get steamed vegetables every day and they couldn't be healthier or happier—so why not give it a try?

69 Think Before You Drink

Our natural forests are truly beautiful and I know many of you enjoy hiking with your dogs in the great outdoors. One hidden hazard you should know about is a disease you and your dog can get by drinking "natural" water from mountain streams and lakes.

Giardiasis is an intestinal disorder caused by a microscopic organism, and it can cause severe discomfort. Symptoms include diarrhea, loss of appetite, abdominal cramps and bloating. Giardiasis can be passed between humans and animals. Dogs, like people, can become infected.

If you are going on an extended trip to the mountains, the best way to treat water is to boil it for at least one minute. At high altitudes (above 10,000 feet), it should be boiled for three to five minutes. For short trips, take a supply of water from home for yourself and your pet. Don't let Fido drink from the streams!

70 Keep A Lid On That Garbage Can

A pet who digs in garbage cans has a habit that is hazardous to his health. Aluminum foil, plastic wrap, corks and other trash that your pet gets into can cause serious injury or death if swallowed. Bones—especially easily splintered ones from fish and poultry—can lodge in the esophagus or cause intestinal damage. Also, cigarette butts can make your pet ill.

Protect your pet by keeping the garbage tightly covered or in a cabinet. Don't reinforce his taste for table scraps by rewarding his begging with leftovers; he may be more likely to look for goodies in the garbage. Call your veterinarian for emergency instructions if you suspect a trash-related tragedy.

Lawnmower Alert

Before you start your mower's engine, take a quick look underneath and inside the bag. Precious felines may be saved from a horrible fate.

---

71 Snail Bait Dangers

During the summer, many of us expose our Best Friends to an extremely dangerous product—snail bait. Whether you choose a granulated or liquid form, you are risking serious, even life-threatening harm to your pet. Excessive drooling, hyperactivity and tremors—especially in the rear legs—are the most frequent indicators of a run-in with this poison. Prompt medical attention can be a matter of life or death.

To avoid this danger, pick up those snails yourself in the early morning. Restricting your water usage to the bare minimum will help discourage snails from visiting your garden. If you feel you must use snail bait, water it into the soil and keep your pets off the area for at least 10 days.

Traveling With Your Pets

72 Traveling With Pets

If you are a member of an auto club, I'm sure you know they provide information about hotels and motels that will accommodate you and your pets. If you aren't a member, however, don't despair. Get a copy of *Pets R Permitted*, a directory of nationwide motels, hotels and bed-and-breakfast inns that accept pets. This is an informative booklet, available through Doris Day Animal League, that also offers tips on traveling and it's updated each year.

A health certificate is an absolute "must" for anyone traveling out of the U.S. with his pet. This certificate is required by federal law. It must be signed by a veterinarian, stating that the animal is in good health and his rabies vaccination is current. And remember this—it must be dated within 10 days of your departure in most states. Check with your county health department for accurate information.

GETTING READY

73 Packing For Your Pet

Your pet's travel kit should include food and water bowls, a can opener, treats, a favorite toy, a blanket and a comb or brush. Take along a scooper and plastic bags or disposable "poop scoopers" (available at pet shops). You still need to clean up after your pet, even when you're traveling.

A special travel tag should have your pet's name, your name and a destination address and phone number. If you don't have a destination number, include the name and number of a friend or relative.

Be certain to carry an up-to-date certificate of vaccination and a health certificate. If your pet has a medical problem, you should carry with you a copy of his medical history to show to a veterinarian if your pet becomes ill while on the road.

Accustom your pet to being on a leash and *always* use it when traveling. Your pet can bolt into traffic or become lost in a strange place if he's not properly restrained.

If your dog or cat is not used to being in the car, use the motion sickness techniques that follow to help him get used to riding along. Take along a favorite blanket and teach him to lie down or sit quietly. Don't let your dog stick his head out of the window. The wind can cause eye irritations and other problems. For safety sake, your best bet is to keep your pet in his pet carrier and take frequent exercise breaks as you travel.

74 Solving Motion Sickness

My four-leggers love to ride in the car. When I go out, I usually take a couple of pals along and they really look forward to these outings.

I've met many people who complain that their pet always becomes sick when they visit the grooming parlor or the veterinarian. This happens because of fear and anxiety. When the animal is stressed, acid pours into the stomach, causing nausea and vomiting.

The answer to this problem is to make the outing a positive experience. If your pet only rides in the car when he's going to the veterinarian or groomer, it's natural to dread the trip.

Accustom your dog or cat to the car slowly. Your cat, of course, should always be in a carrier when riding in the car, so put the carrier inside without even starting the engine. Just leave it on the seat for a few minutes and talk reassuringly to your kitty-cat. Turn on the radio and find some pleasant music. Leave the doors open and let him walk through the car a couple of times with the doors open.

When the dog seems comfortable moving about the car, close the doors and again reassure. Next, start the engine; drive a very short distance, perhaps to the end of the driveway and back; then go to the end of the block; next, drive around the block. The key is to gradually increase the time in the car.

Although I've explained it briefly, this desensitization process takes time. It may take a few days, or even weeks, for you to move from sitting in the car to actually driving down the block. Your pet will let you know when he feels comfortable to move on.

Above all, be patient. This is a problem that can be solved.

In severe cases, anti-motion sickness preparations such as Dramamine or Bonine can be used. Contact your veterinarian for specific dosage information.

75 Kitty Carriers

Cats don't like to stay still in a strange place, and they can be difficult to control. If they are startled, their caregiver can be badly scratched, and if the door happens to be open at that time, the kitty-cat may escape.

I've found that it's absolutely essential to transport cats in a carrier when going to the veterinarian, or on any adventure away from home. The airline-type kennels are better because they have adequate ventilation, they're sturdy and safe, and your cat can have a peek at his surroundings. Cats feel secure in a carrier and I wouldn't be without one—or two or three.

76 **Cats In The Car**

If you are on a lengthy trip and you feel the need to let your kitty-cat stretch his legs, be sure to use a well-fitting harness and leash—not a collar from which he can easily free himself.

Cats often can't relax enough to use a litter box in the car, but they may be desperate by the time you take a rest stop. Feeding small amounts at a time during a long trip will help to keep kitty's tummy settled.

Cats can travel safely and in relative comfort if you plan ahead, so buckle up, confine your cat and happy traveling!

If you have two kitty-cats and they get along well, consider one large carrier that they can comfortably travel in together. Your cats will feel more at ease, being able to curl up next to each other as they do at home. They'll also be able to groom and comfort each other to relieve anxiety.

77 Build A Pet Lift

Medical problems and old-age symptoms can make getting into a car difficult, painful and dangerous for both you and your pet. An ideal solution to this problem is a ramp that you can build yourself. This is a simple project that can easily be accomplished one Saturday morning.

You'll need a piece of 3/4 inch plywood about 2-1/2 feet wide and 4-1/2 feet long. Use a staple gun to attach a carpet runner to help keep your pet from slipping. Attach two or three shelf brackets at one end of the ramp so that you can hook the ramp over your car bumper (if it's a hatchback or station wagon) or side door. Your pet should be able to walk right into your vehicle. The ramp will slide easily into the back of a station wagon or into the trunk of most cars.

If your pet isn't in need, how about making a ramp for the pet of a friend or relative? It's a simple way to show you care.

78 Petsitters

If you find that your pet is just not the traveling kind, it's important to have someone come to your home who will care for your pet, plants and home with tender loving care. You can find bonded petsitters through your veterinarian or a listing in the phone book. You may want to ask among your friends—you might find someone who'd love to care for your four-legger while you're away.

Be sure to leave detailed information about your pet's daily routine. Write down what he eats, how often he eats, how he should be exercised, what medications/vitamins he takes, and how to reach your regular veterinarian and an emergency veterinarian. Leave your travel itinerary and set an agreed upon time, in advance, to telephone home and check conditions. Be sure that your pet is wearing a comfortable nylon collar with an ID tag.

A vacation can be a positive experience for your pet—even if he spends it at home. The extra attention he'll receive from his "sitter" will be a real treat and he'll have the added joy of welcoming you home.

Acquiring or Losing a Pet

A NEW FAMILY MEMBER COMES HOME

79 Pet Adoption

Surprisingly, many people begin their search for a pet without taking stock of their situation. Before you decide to bring a pet into your home, you must first decide why you want a pet. Are you looking for a lifelong responsibility, a friend and companion— or do you want an alarm system? (If the latter is true, call a security system company.)

The next question is, will it be a dog or a cat? By their nature, cats are a bit easier to handle. They absolutely must be kept indoors to keep them safe from other animals, humans and disease. They should have toys and scratch posts to keep them occupied and out of mischief. And if someone won't be home during the day, I recommend taking *two* cats to keep each other company.

If a dog is what you're looking for, consider your

circumstances. Again, will someone be home during the day? If not, your dog will be lonely, and that's how mischievous behavior starts. Digging, chewing and barking are all signs of boredom and loneliness, so think about adopting *two* if your pet will be home alone for hours on end. Two dogs will become best friends and companions. They'll get great exercise by romping together and that in turn will keep them fit, vital and healthy.

The very first thing I look for when I'm placing a dog is a safe yard. Fencing must be six feet high even if I'm placing a small dog. It's just as important to keep other dogs out as it is to keep your dog in.

All gates must be padlocked. Too many pets stray from their homes because a gate was left open by a child, gardener or utility person.

If you are thinking about adopting a dog you should have a doggy door. It will give your pet a certain amount of freedom and allow him to make some very important decisions on the spur of the moment. Kitchens and utility rooms are ideal places for a doggy door. If that's not possible, install one in your garage so that your pet will always have shelter from extreme weather conditions.

Even if your new dog has had previous obedience training, it's a great idea to attend some classes so you and your new friend can learn to work together. It's a wonderful way to bond, and you'll be delighted to see how willing and eager your pet is to please.

When you're thinking about adopting a new pet, be realistic about your expectations and time limitations. Remember, this will be a lifetime responsibility and it requires careful planning and commitment.

80 Living Gifts

Although the thought of surprising someone special with a gift of a four-legged friend seems like a terrific idea, the holidays are a particularly difficult time to introduce a new pet into a household. All of the things we love about the holiday season—the visitors, the sparkling lights and shiny ornaments, the excitement and the commotion—can be very confusing and frightening to a little newcomer.

If you decide to give someone special the gift of a new pet, why not give him the gift of choosing as well? How about presenting a gift certificate from your local SPCA or shelter? Make your own greeting card with a verse you've written about your idea. Or buy some of the items the new pet will need—like bowls, food, brushes, toys, a litter box—and wrap them as gifts along with your "note of intent."

Choosing a pet is an important decision and a very personal one, so let the caregiver-to-be select just the right pet at just the right time—when the holiday commotion is over.

81 Introducing A Second Dog Into Your Household

Thinking of enlarging your canine family? Through my work with the Doris Day Pet Foundation, I've had the opportunity to meet many wonderful people who've adopted our precious orphans. Although I never press them to adopt more than one pet, experience has shown me that it's best to have two. Introducing a new dog into your family must be done carefully to avoid hard feelings and to get the relationship off to a good start.

Once you decide to add another dog to your family, consider these questions:

• What age should the new dog be?

- What sex should the new dog be?
- What size can the new dog be as compared to the resident dog?

What age should the new dog be?

Puppies are hard to resist, but they are a lot of work! They require proper training and socialization, and that will take a lot of your time. They eat 3-4 times a day and if you work, it's either inconvenient or impossible to get home for the feedings. A young adult dog (10 months-2 years) is more settled than a puppy and is usually over his crying and chewing stages. He is a "teenager" full of energy, eager to please, and somewhat rebellious.

The adult dog (2 years and older) tends to be easygoing and mature. In fact, "older" dogs can be much easier to please than puppies. Prospective caregivers often overlook a more mature dog because they want younger dogs they can mold and shape and they want a dog who will be with them for many years. The adult dog is just as adaptable as a pup, and with the continuing advances in medical care, knowledge of a proper diet and the right nurturing, an adult dog will live to a ripe old age. Many of my "angels" live to be in their twenties, I'm happy to report.

What sex should the dog be?

Often, two neutered males or two spayed females will get along just fine. Their ability to get along really depends a lot on their personalities and the way you handle their introduction. Of course, with a few exceptions, a male and female (neutered and spayed, of course) will become great friends and there shouldn't be any problems.

What size should the new dog be compared to the resident dog?

The size of the second dog will also determine how the two dogs will get along. If there is a considerable difference in size, the dogs may enjoy each other's company, but may not be able to roughhouse. If the resident dog is a senior citizen, a low-key dog of almost any size would be fine. The younger your dog, the nicer it would be to have a frisky companion.

After you've decided to adopt a second dog and have made your choice, it's time to think about the introductions. This should always be done away from your house because some dogs will view the newcomer as a threat.

Arrange for a friend to bring the new dog to a nearby park to meet with you and your own dog. Both dogs should be on a lead, so just walk up to each other casually and let the dogs get acquainted. There may be some posturing, and it isn't unusual to hear some growling and barking. If things start to get out of control, separate the dogs with a firm, "NO! That's enough!" When they've calmed down (still on leads), let them walk around a little, then let them play again.

When they've tired, take them home. Keep the new dog on a lead as you show him around. Take him outside to the area where the resident dog relieves himself. Show the new dog where his food and water bowls are. If you have a pet door, put the new dog through it a couple of times.

The first week is the most difficult, and you should supervise the dogs for the first few days. Don't leave them alone until you're sure they're getting along. Also, you should feed them separately to avoid fights over food. In fact, you may always have to stand between them while they eat and may even have to put their dishes down at opposite ends of the room. This is the safest way to feed them. Believe me, I know from experience.

It's important that you give each dog some kind of individual attention. Time alone can be as simple as brushing one dog while the other dog is occupied. It could be an individual trip to the park, a game of hide-and-seek, or a bit of obedience work.

Once the initial adjustment is over, you can relax and enjoy both of your dogs. Having two dogs may seem to be twice the work, but it's really easier. Having two children is easier than having one because they entertain each other so they don't get bored. Also, having two dogs will double your companionship, fun and love. Don't be afraid—try it. You'll love it!

82 An Easter Reminder

During the Easter season, we begin to see signs along country roads and in pet shops: "Bunnies, chicks and ducklings for sale." I shudder every time I think of the untold numbers of Easter "presents" that are given with every good intention, only to be discarded weeks or months later—if they live that long.

Animals aren't expendable items to be tossed aside when they grow too large or rambunctious or when the owner simply loses interest. Whether your Best Friend is a turtle, fish, snake, gerbil, hamster or rat, a cat or dog, or any other non-human critter, they are a lifelong responsibility and commitment.

Bunnies, chicks and ducklings grow up to be rabbits, chickens and ducks. Each year, many thousands are dumped in isolated areas to fend for themselves after their cuteness has worn off.

Please, buy a cuddly stuffed animal instead.

83 Rabbits As Pets

If you're thinking about adopting a bunny, there's a lot you should know before you make a decision.

First, visit the library and read about rabbits. There are many excellent books that will tell you all you need to know.

A common complaint is that the precious baby bunny who was so cute and cuddly a few months ago has become a terror. Rabbits are sexually mature at around five months of age and they are considered adults at around one year. As they mature, they may undergo a drastic personality change. Their behavior becomes unpredictable and they may bite or scratch. The solution is simple: spay or neuter and they will revert back to their lovable, sweet selves.

Rabbits don't usually make good pets for young children. Adult rabbits don't really enjoy cuddling and they can be seriously hurt if they're not handled properly.

Rabbits are very easy to feed. All of their nutritional requirements can be met by feeding cereals, green foods and vegetables. Don't feed candy!

A rabbit needs lots of exercise, and outdoor exercise is better than indoor exercise. A good idea is to fence off a section of your yard. That way your bunny is contained with ample room to play.

Most rabbits need a companion rabbit to be happy. Single rabbits are likely to be bored and therefore more likely to get into trouble. I always say, two is better than one!

Properly cared for rabbits live 6–10 years, so don't make a hasty decision. Once you adopt a rabbit, as with any pet, you must be willing to make a life-long commitment.

84 **Parakeets As Pets**

Parakeets, or budgies, make wonderful companions. They're easy to care for and are ideal as a "first" pet. Since they spend virtually their entire lives in a cage, it's important to make their home as comfortable as possible. Remember that a parakeet doesn't need vertical height. A wise friend once explained to me that parakeets are airplanes, not helicopters! Their space needs to be spread out because they enjoy most moving horizontally from perch to perch.

According to the ornithology lab at Cornell University, for small birds, the cage size should be 2 to 8 cubic feet (length x height x width); for medium birds, 12 to 18 cubic feet, and for large birds, 24 to 36 cubic feet. Location is very important. Keep parakeets away from drafts and temperature extremes, like east or west facing windows. Cover the cage at night with a towel (fasten with a clothespin or "chip clip") or purchase a cover from a pet supply store.

Perches should be of varying diameters. Parakeets can suffer from foot problems if their little feet are clamped, day after day, in the same position. Also, sandpaper perches can hurt their feet. Wood perches are best.

Baths are wonderful. For a change of pace, you can hang a bath on the inside of the cage for a little while each day. Don't provide too many toys or the cage will be cluttered and your bird won't be able to move around. Put clean newspaper or paper towels on the cage bottom each day.

Many experts feel grit (a bird gravel) helps to grind up food in the parakeet's stomach, but this is a controversial issue. Check with your veterinarian.

Cuttle bones are great. They provide minerals and iodine and help keep beaks filed. Besides standard food found in pet supply shops, parakeets like lettuce (romaine and iceberg), fresh fruit, carrots and crackers. Broccoli is wonderful and they love it. Clips are available at pet supply shops to hold these goodies against the cage, at the end of a perch.

Your veterinarian should have a look at your new pet to be sure he's healthy. See the doctor immediately if you notice any signs of illness like frequent sneezing, loss of appetite, or lethargy. Enjoy your feathered friend!

85 Bird Boredom

If you notice that your bird is particularly noisy or is pulling the feathers out of his chest, boredom may be a problem. You may be tempted to deal with the noise by covering his cage or simply ignoring him, but neither of these choices should satisfy either you or your bird.

Even if your bird is older, a pal could be the answer. To increase the chances that they'll get along, you should choose the opposite sex to what you already have.

We all need a friend, and another bird could make a major difference in your feathered friend's life.

86 How About A Hamster?

Hamsters make great "entry level" pets, especially for children. They're low maintenance and they occupy only a small area. They're very affectionate and playful, so children can get used to handling them and learn to be responsible for their care and well-being.

I recommend that you adopt a baby hamster and get him used to being handled—gently and carefully. Check with your local shelter. They often have hamsters, rabbits and other pets available for adoption to a loving home. A grown hamster may bite if he becomes nervous or excited and that could easily happen in new surroundings. Also, hamsters are escape artists, so you will learn that part of the responsibility of caring for a pet is keeping him safe.

87 **Breeding A Pet**

When puppies and kittens are on the way, it should be a wonderful learning experience for the whole family. It is truly a time for learning, but not the learning one might think.

In today's world, breeding a dog or cat creates anything but a wonderful experience. What families learn many times is that there aren't any homes out there for puppies and kittens who grow up to be dogs and cats.

Pet overpopulation has reached epidemic proportions. Humane societies and shelters destroy more than *10 million* dogs and cats each year! That number comprises between 15 and 25 percent of our entire domestic animal population. Yes, one out of every four or five pets is destroyed each year because there are no homes.

Other animals who aren't killed by the humane society are simply abandoned on the side of a road or released into an urban environment to fend for themselves. We have all seen these sad and pitiful creatures, unable to find food, or victimized by insensitive youth or teenagers.

Of course, shelters and humane societies do try to find homes for the animals, and that is where many of us adopted our own pets. But with the homes not there, a large percentage of healthy, adoptable and loving animals are killed—or worse yet, turned over for animal research.

Children may be excited about preparing for the births, but a terrible reality lies ahead. Is the lesson of "witnessing a birth" more important than the suffering those kittens or puppies must endure because nobody wants them? As responsible parents, we have the opportunity to set an example of compassion and sensitivity towards all living creatures. That is the most important lesson we can teach our children.

PLACING AN ANIMAL

88 Lost And Found

What can you do when you find a stray animal? The answer must come from your heart. It's easy to call the SPCA and let someone else take care of the problem. But can you simply walk away, assuming that your little foundling will survive? What if the owner isn't found? What if the last day arrives and no one has adopted that precious four-legger?

Animal rescue work takes time, energy and commitment. The enormous problem of too many pets and not enough homes can only be solved if we *all* work together. The commitment must come from government agencies, private organizations and every individual who cares.

If you find a stray animal, *please* do your part to help. Local laws may require that you take him to the SPCA or municipal shelter—but your responsibility doesn't have to end there. First of all, ask for the animal's impound number. With that number, you can call the shelter to inquire about the animal. And if he has been injured, be certain he receives proper medical attention.

Make every effort to locate the owner. Check the lost ads in your newspaper and watch for notices posted in the area where you found the animal.

If all efforts fail and the animal has not been claimed or adopted, you have a wonderful opportunity to save a little life. Destiny may have given you the greatest friend you'll ever have. And if it just doesn't work for you, there is someone out there waiting. Talk to friends and family. Write a terrific ad and have a list of questions ready to ask a potential new guardian.

Rescue work is tough but very rewarding, so don't look the other way the next time you see a frightened, bewildered four-legger trying to find his way home. Roll up your sleeves and accept the challenge . . . you'll be glad you did!

89 Placing Your Pet

Sometimes, despite our best efforts, we need to find a new home for our Best Friend. Following are some tips on finding a new home for your dog by running an ad in the newspaper.

First—check with everyone you know who might provide a lead to a new, loving home. Ask relatives, friends, co-workers, your veterinarian and your mail carrier. Take a nice picture of your pet, write a clever, brief description and see if you can post it at your office, your church or your veterinarian's office.

Then write a great ad, something with emotion that will make people want to see your pet. For example, "Precious German Shepherd mix, neutered male, desperately needs loving home. All shots, house-trained, perfect family pet, free to best home." Hopefully, you'll get some good calls, but I won't mislead you— there are *thousands* of homeless pets out there and not many good homes.

When interviewing prospective owners over the phone, I get a feeling about the person right away. It has to do with his tone of voice, sincerity and interest, and responses to my questions.

   1. "Are you familiar with this breed?"

      Generally speaking, most breeds have certain inherent characteristics. For instance, Terriers tend to be a bit hyper and feisty and may not be too pleased with an active toddler as a playmate. The same goes for Cocker Spaniels. Labs and Retrievers, on the other hand, tend to be calm, patient and gentle. They make excellent family pets. It's important for your caller to be familiar with the breed.

2. "Do you have children? What are their ages?" You ask this for the reasons stated above. Also, if you're placing a puppy, it's not a good idea to place him in a family with small children. It could be dangerous for the puppy.

3. "Is your yard fenced? How high is the fencing?" It's important to have *at least* a 6' fence, and one that is well-built, not rickety and ready to fall down! If your dog is an escape artist, you must let the caller know.

4. "Where will the dog sleep?" If the answer is, "In the doghouse on the patio," it's the wrong answer. They should all have a warm, cozy bed indoors.

5. "Will someone be home during the day? Where will the dog be when you're not there?" Lots of people go home for lunch to spend some time with their pets. If your caller works, be aware that your pet will probably be alone for at least nine hours each day. Ask the caller if he could get home at lunch time to give the dog treats, play a little ball in the yard, and give him

some attention. It's a nice break for your four-legger who sits alone all day, waiting.

6. "Do you have a doggie door?"

This is a must! It's important for your dog to be a part of the family, to be able to go in and out.

7. "How many dogs and cats have you owned?"

We've heard, "Oh lots. Some got hit by cars and one was stolen,"—wrong answer! This isn't the right home for your beloved pet.

If your caller answers your questions with the honesty and sincerity you're looking for, the next step is a visit. Invite the prospective owner to your home to meet your pet. That way your dog will be seen where he's most comfortable and he'll look his best. It will really give the potential guardian a chance to see how the dog reacts in his own surroundings.

LOSING A PET

90 Dealing With The Loss Of A Pet

As much as we hate even thinking about it, the death of a pet is something we all eventually have to face. Whether you've shared a long, happy life together or you've been best friends and companions for a short time, saying good-bye is a terribly sad thing to face.

Sometimes it seems that the pain just won't end

and many people say they'll never have another pet. That's when you must put aside your own feelings, forget about "self" and think about taking another little life into your home. Everyone grieves in his own way and some take longer to heal than others, but there's no better way to begin the healing journey than to find another little soul who needs you.

I have pictures of my angels—past and present—all around the house and it helps me to see their sweet faces. I remember all of the joy they brought to my life and I dwell on the happiness that I gave to them. It warms my heart to know that I was able to save them from abandonment and give them so much love and goodness. They had the best, and knowing that uplifts my thoughts because they didn't want for anything. With those thoughts in mind, I'm able to get past my grief and help others in need. Thank goodness I'm in a position to help more and more—because they just keep rolling in!

Following are three books that may help you deal with the loss of a pet. If you can't find them on the shelves, contact the publisher or ask your bookstore to place a special order for you.

Joy in a Wooly Cat, Julie Adams Church, (HJ Kramer Inc., Dept. DF, P O Box 1082 Tiburon, CA 94920; 1987)

When Your Pet Dies, James Quackenbush, M.S.W., and Denise Graveline, (Simon & Schuster, Dept. DF,

1230 Avenue of the Americas, New York, NY 10020;
1985)

Pet Loss and Human Bereavement, W.J. Key, H.A.
Nieburg, A.H. Kutscher, F.M. Grey and C.E. Fudin,
(Iowa State University Press, Dept. DF, Ames, IA
50010; 1984).

91 Pet Theft

In days gone by, a collar and identification tag
would most certainly ensure that your phone would
ring if your Best Friend managed to slip out of your
yard and take a stroll around the neighborhood. These
days, it isn't enough to simply tag your pet because
if he gets out, it may be because of a dognapper.
Believe it or not, the crime of dognapping is on the
rise and family pets are being sold for profit.

They may be sold to a research facility, or held for
a reward, or they may be sold to an unsuspecting
third party. They may be transported hundreds of
miles from their homes and if they escape, as they
sometimes do, they wander the streets totally bewildered, pitifully searching for their families.

The best protection for your Best Friend is a safe
yard with high fences and locked gates. You may
want to ask your veterinarian about "microchipping"
your pet. A small microchip implant can be scanned
by a research facility or shelter if your Best Friend

ends up there. The microchip may be his only link home. Your doggy is probably as trusting and naive as a "two-legged toddler" so with that in mind, keep an eye on your four-legger. Above all, don't let him wander the streets by himself.

PET ABUSE

92 Animal Cruelty

Over the years, I've received literally hundreds of letters and calls from people who have observed mistreatment of animals. Some describe neglect, others complain of abuse, and many report out-and-out cruelty. They all want to help but they don't know how to go about it.

My advice is always the same—contact the SPCA and file a complaint. Their specially-trained investigators know the laws protecting animals and they will determine if there is a violation.

Many forms of mistreatment occur simply because owners are uneducated about the proper care of their four-legged friend. They may provide the requisite food, water, shelter and little else. Their dog may spend his life outdoors and have minimal or no contact with the family or other animals. He may become noisy or destructive out of boredom, causing neighbors to become alarmed or angry. These neighbors may then contact the authorities.

Although the dog is technically being properly cared for, there is much that could be done to ameliorate the situation and make the dog more comfortable. If the law is not being broken, the investigator will still make suggestions to alleviate the problem. He will also attempt to make follow-up visits to check on the situation.

Index by Section–Volume 1

Become a Member of The Doris Day Animal League

The Doris Day Animal League exists to increase the public's awareness of its responsibility to animals through legislative initiatives, public and membership education, and to ensure the adherence to regulations already enacted to protect animals.

Because public support is so critical to our work, the Doris Day Animal League keeps its membership cost at just $10. Members receive a one year subscription to DDAL's *Animal Guardian* magazine, updates on animal-related issues, and the opportunity to let your elected officials know how you feel about animal issues.

To become a member of the Doris Day Animal League, simply fill out the form below and return it, along with at least a $10 membership contribution, to Doris Day Animal League, 227 Massachusetts Avenue, NE, Suite 100, Washington, D.C. 20002.

Name: _____

Address: _____

City: _____

State: _____ Zip code: _____

____ My check is enclosed

____ Please charge my credit card: __ MasterCard __ VISA

number: ☐☐☐☐☐☐☐☐☐☐☐☐☐☐☐☐ exp date: _____

Signature: _____

Thank You

Contributions to the Doris Day Animal League are not tax-deductible. This is because the law does not permit a deduction for contributions to any organization primarily engaged in lobbying for legislation.